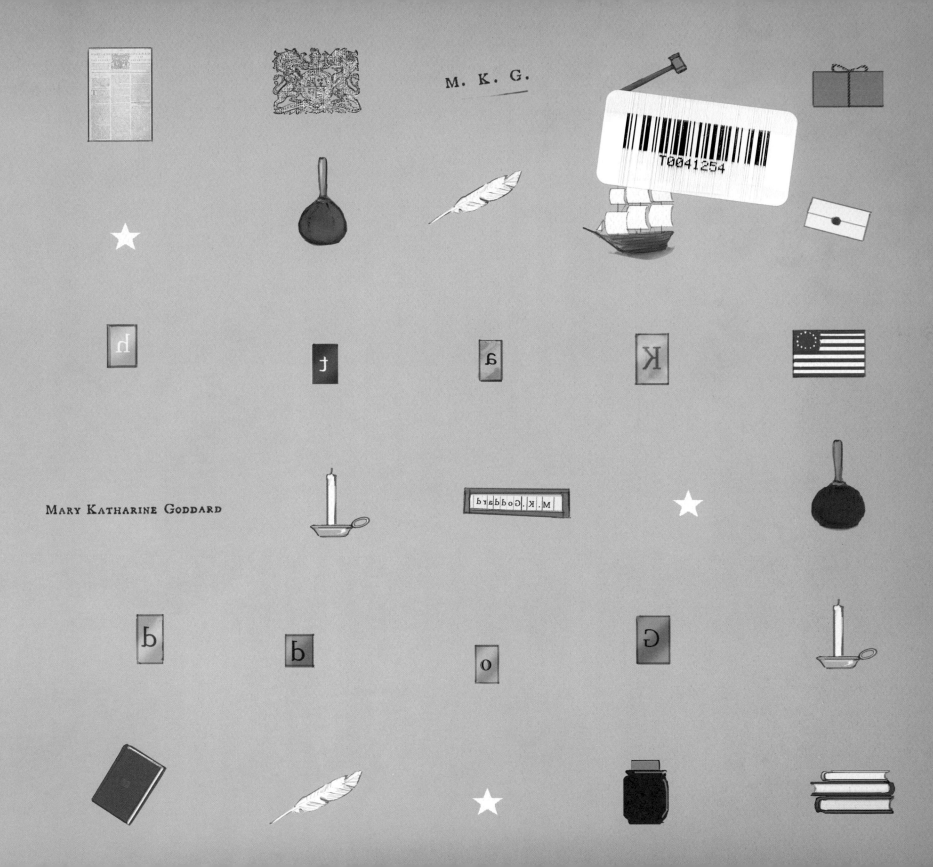

M. K. G.

MARY KATHARINE GODDARD

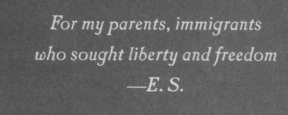

*For my parents, immigrants
who sought liberty and freedom*
—E. S.

For my friend Jin
—D. P.

ABOUT THIS BOOK

The illustrations for this book were created digitally in Adobe Photoshop with scans of watercolors and textures. This book was edited by Christy Ottaviano and designed by Patrick Collins. The production was supervised by Lillian Sun, and the production editor was Annie McDonnell. The text was set in Caslon Antique, and the display type is Caslon Antique.

HER NAME WAS MARY KATHARINE

THE ONLY WOMAN WHOSE NAME IS ON THE DECLARATION OF INDEPENDENCE

ELLA SCHWARTZ

Illustrated by DOW PHUMIRUK

Christy Ottaviano Books

LITTLE, BROWN AND COMPANY
New York   Boston

BEFORE AMERICA was even a country, a young girl lived in the colony of Connecticut in a busy port town with her parents and younger brother. News from near and far would arrive with each docked ship. She grew up under British rule, learning to love the colonies she would one day fight for.

Her name was Mary Katharine Goddard.

Most parents in colonial America thought girls should only learn to cook, sew, and take care of the house, but Mary Katharine's parents disagreed. They wanted their daughter to have the same education as her brother, William. Mary Katharine learned how to read and write just as well as her brother. They were mostly taught by their mother, who encouraged the Goddard children to study Latin, ancient history, and classic literature. As a young girl, Mary Katharine realized that knowledge made her powerful.

Mary Katharine and her brother were only teenagers when their father died. William was in the process of apprenticing as a printer, an important and well-respected job. Their mother decided to move with Mary Katharine to Providence, Rhode Island, to start a new life.

After finishing his apprenticeship, William used his family's money to open his own printshop and launched Providence's first newspaper, the *Providence Gazette, and Country Journal*. William wasn't the best newspaper owner—he was more interested in traveling and making friends with important people. He thought Providence was dull.

But Mary Katharine and her mom loved Providence. Since William was often away or preoccupied, they couldn't rely on him to keep the family business running. So, by the age of twenty-four, when most young colonial women were thinking about marriage and children, Mary Katharine was learning how to be a printer—composing pages, setting type, and operating the press.

Mary Katharine knew the importance of this work. In colonial America, printers were the primary way people received information about what was happening in their community and the world around them.

By 1765, anger against Britain erupted within the colonies. Britain announced the Stamp Act, which forced colonists to pay a tax on printed paper. The colonists didn't think this was fair. They called it "taxation without representation," because they had no representation in Parliament to vote for or against the tax. Many colonists protested, and the *Providence Gazette* was no exception, printing articles complaining about the Stamp Act.

PROVIDENCE
GAZETTE

Eventually, William decided he'd had enough of Providence. He left the printshop in the hands of Mary Katharine and moved to Philadelphia, Pennsylvania, to start another newspaper called the *Pennsylvania Chronicle, and Universal Advertiser*.

Providence

Philadelphia

Baltimore

Running the *Pennsylvania Chronicle* was
hard work, and William was easily distracted.
But someone had to keep the business going.
William decided the solution was to sell the
Providence paper and he convinced Mary
Katharine and his mother to move to
Philadelphia. Up for the challenge and
always loyal, Mary Katharine joined
her brother to work on the
Pennsylvania Chronicle.

Soon William chose to move again. This time he headed to Baltimore, Maryland, where he started another newspaper called the *Maryland Journal, and the Baltimore Advertiser*. It came as no surprise six months later when he closed the *Pennsylvania Chronicle* and asked Mary Katharine to come run his new paper.

Her name was Mary Katharine and she would not let her brother down.

By then tensions were heating up between the colonies and Britain. They had a wide ocean between them and disagreed about how the colonies should be governed. Many colonists felt they should no longer be ruled by Britain.

The British did everything possible to hold their power over the colonies.

While William preoccupied himself with other business, Mary Katharine kept the *Maryland Journal* going, printing important news about British conflicts. She had strong opinions and printed bold commentaries, making clear she did not like Britain's unfair treatment of the colonies.

Her name was Mary Katharine and she had important news to print.

It is the misfortune of all countries, that they sooner or later lie under the unhappy necessity to defend themselves by arms against the ambition of their Governors, and to fight for what is their own.

If we can tax the Americans without their consent, they have…nothing which they can call their own.

Liberty with danger, is preferable to servitude, with security.

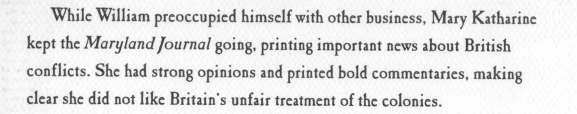

> We will strain every nerve, and brave every danger, to stimulate our countrymen on this side the Atlantic...

> A British parliament has no more right to tax an American in anything than they have the right to tax the people in Japan...

While Mary Katharine was successfully running her brother's printing business, things weren't going as well for William. He often got into fights expressing his strong opinions about politics and British rule.

Then things got worse for William. While visiting his former home of Philadelphia, William was arrested and sent to jail. He had failed to pay the bills he ran up while publishing the *Pennsylvania Chronicle*.

On April 19, 1775, shots rang out in Lexington and Concord. This was the "shot heard round the world," and it marked the beginning of the Revolutionary War. The *Maryland Journal* was one of the first papers in the colonies to report that the war had begun.

The Revolutionary War was a difficult time for the colonies. Food and resources were scarce, and people worried about keeping their families safe.

The printing business suffered, but Mary Katharine understood the importance of getting information out to the people. Throughout the war, she rarely missed an edition.

Her name was Mary Katharine and she was a patriot.

Mary Katharine couldn't rely on William anymore. She knew that if it weren't for her, the *Maryland Journal* would not be the important paper that it was. Just one month before her thirty-seventh birthday, she decided it was finally time to take credit for her hard work.

She changed the paper's ownership information to read:

Published by M. K. GODDARD

This was a daring move. Finally, she was announcing to the world that she was the real genius behind the paper, not William. But she chose to use her initials, M. K., so that readers couldn't tell whether the publisher of the paper was a man or a woman. Since women were only expected to run a household—certainly not a business— some people may not have realized a woman was behind the respected newspaper.

Her name was Mary Katharine.
But she wasn't ready yet
to announce it to the world.

William may not have been a very good newspaperman, but he liked making deals and dabbling in politics. While Mary Katharine was busy running William's papers, William was working on a project of his own—a colonial postal system to replace the British-controlled mail service. After the Continental Congress approved his system, Mary Katharine was named the first postmaster of Baltimore and the first woman postmaster in the thirteen colonies.

This was an important responsibility. Baltimore was a bustling port city, and its post office would become one of the busiest in all the colonies.

Mary Katharine took her job as postmaster very seriously, but she never neglected the *Maryland Journal*. Now, more than ever, the people needed the press, especially with hostilities rising between the colonies and Britain.

On July 4, 1776, a handwritten version of the Declaration of Independence was approved by the Continental Congress, declaring freedom from the British. Copies were hastily printed and distributed. The declaration was read in public squares, in taverns, and on the battlefields in celebration of liberty.

Except the names of the signers never appeared on the document.

There was good reason for this. The Declaration of Independence was an act of treason against Britain. If the British learned the identities of the signers, they could be sentenced to death.

The war raged on, and the Continental Congress moved to Baltimore, just a few short blocks from Mary Katharine's printing office. Mary Katharine had the responsibility of overseeing the delegates' mail, printing congressional documents, and running a newspaper.

The *Maryland Journal* became a pipeline of information for the American people. Mary Katharine knew a free and open press would be an important part of the America that was beginning to form.

And then the Continental Congress made a daring decision—to print a new version of the Declaration of Independence. This time with all the names of the signers.

Congress gave the job of designing and printing this official document to a trusted fellow patriot—Mary Katharine.

Mary Katharine had been handed a great honor and a big responsibility. Her printed version of the Declaration of Independence would announce the birth of a new nation and was intended to be preserved forever for future generations. The people named on the document pledged their honor, fortunes, and lives in the formation of the United States of America. If the war was lost, every person named on that document would be sentenced to death.

Her name was Mary Katharine and she had an important job to do.

Mary Katharine carefully selected a design for the Declaration of Independence and skillfully set all the letters on her press. There was just one last detail needed before she started her printing machines.

At the very bottom, Mary Katharine added her name to the document. She knew the risk. By adding her name, she was putting her life in danger. But that didn't matter. Mary Katharine wanted the world to know that being a patriot was a sacrifice worth dying for.

This time, when the stakes were at their highest, Mary Katharine did not hesitate.

This time she did not shy away from using her full name.

BALTIMORE, in MARYLAND: Printed by MARY KATHARINE GODDARD.

Her name was
Mary Katharine Goddard.
And her name is the only woman's name
that appears on an official copy of
the Declaration of Independence.

Author's Note

WHEN I TELL FRIENDS AND COLLEAGUES that I wrote a book about the only woman whose name appears on an official copy of the Declaration of Independence, the first reaction I get is a blank stare. After a few beats I hear, "But there is no woman's name on the Declaration of Independence." I myself had the exact same response when I first learned about Mary Katharine Goddard. And yet, her name has always been there.

I wondered how it was possible that Mary Katharine Goddard's name appears on our nation's most treasured document, but I had never heard of her. When I began my research, I realized how selective history can be. Surely, a woman whose name is memorialized on the Declaration of Independence should be honored for generations. But that wasn't the case. In fact, Mary Katharine Goddard is barely recognized in history. Not a single portrait of her is known to exist. Very few of her personal records have been preserved. The quotes included in this book's illustrations are actual quotes from newspapers Mary Katharine printed, and while we cannot know for sure if these are Mary Katharine's own words, we do know that by printing them she was endorsing them as her own. There is even confusion over the spelling of her name: Katharine, Katherine, and even Katy. It's not clear why she used so many different name variations, but for this book

I chose the spelling *Katharine*, which is how she wrote it on her most lasting legacy, the Declaration of Independence.

Yet much has been written about her brother, William Goddard. It is true that being a newspaperman was never William's calling. He was easily distracted and often unreliable. But he cared a great deal about colonial politics. In the period leading up to the Revolutionary War, patriots feared British authorities were spying on colonists by intercepting their mail. William realized that the colonies needed an alternative to the British-controlled postal system. This became his life's work. William laid the foundation for the United States Postal Service.

When the Continental Congress finally adopted William's idea for the postal system, William felt he deserved the top job. He had fought for years to promote his vision for mail delivery. But the Continental Congress awarded the job of postmaster general to Benjamin Franklin. To add insult to injury, Franklin awarded his son-in-law the second-in-command position. Goddard was offered the post of surveyor, inspecting post offices and the security of postal routes. While this was an important position, it didn't come with the same prestige. William reluctantly took the job.

His sister, Mary Katharine, was named postmaster of

Baltimore in October 1775. Now in addition to all her printshop duties—selecting and editing articles, setting type, as well as handling advertising, circulation, and accounting—Mary Katharine would be in charge of overseeing one of the busiest post offices in the colonies.

William didn't last long as surveyor. After less than a year, he quit and came back to Baltimore and Mary Katharine. In the shadow of his own failures, it must have annoyed him greatly to see how successful his sister had become. He took back the *Maryland Journal* and removed his sister from the business altogether.

This must have been a major blow to Mary Katharine. She had built the *Maryland Journal* into one of the most respected newspapers in the country. At least Mary Katharine still had the job of Baltimore's postmaster. She continued to run that office until 1789, when the postmaster general decided to remove her from the position, claiming the job was too much for a woman to handle. This was, of course, nonsense, because Mary Katharine had been successfully running the post office for fourteen years. Her neighbors in Baltimore agreed. They organized a petition with over two hundred signatures, demanding the postmaster general reinstate her. When he failed to respond, Mary Katharine took her case to President George Washington, who declined to intervene.

Mary Katharine no longer had the newspaper or the post office. More tragically, she no longer had a relationship with her brother. The bond between them never recovered after William's hostilities. She lived out her remaining days in Baltimore, quietly running a bookshop.

Mary Katharine had an enslaved person, Belinda Starling, who helped her run her business and household. Mary Katharine never married and died at the age of seventy-eight. Her will mentions only one person: Belinda Starling, to whom she granted freedom and left all her possessions.

It is obvious Mary Katharine was a courageous patriot. In writing this book, I often wondered how she must have felt as she prepared the Declaration of Independence for printing. When she set the words "all men are created equal" did she ever stop to think all men *and all women* are created equal? I have no doubt that by choosing to print her full name on the Declaration of Independence, rather than her usual initials, she was making a bold statement that she, a Daughter of Liberty, loved her country as fiercely as any of the Founding Fathers.

Important Terms

BATTLES OF LEXINGTON AND CONCORD: The Battles of Lexington and Concord in the colony of Massachusetts marked the official start of the Revolutionary War. They occurred on April 19, 1775. Later, the famous writer Ralph Waldo Emerson called the start of the war the "shot heard round the world."

COLONY: Territory occupied and governed by another country. Before the United States of America was formed, there were thirteen British colonies in North America. These thirteen colonies joined together to fight against Britain. After the Revolutionary War and the signing of the Declaration of Independence, they became the United States of America. Sometimes, the original thirteen colonies are also referred to as the original thirteen states.

CONTINENTAL CONGRESS: The American government during the Revolutionary War. Delegates from all thirteen colonies were represented.

DECLARATION OF INDEPENDENCE: A statement written by the Continental Congress announcing that the thirteen colonies were no longer under British rule. The Declaration of Independence symbolized the start of a new nation, the United States of America.

PATRIOT: A person who loves and defends their country. At the time of the Revolutionary War, a patriot was a colonist who spoke out or rebelled against the British.

POSTMASTER: Someone in charge of the local post office.

REVOLUTIONARY WAR: The war fought between the thirteen colonies in North America and Britain from 1775 to 1783. Also known as the American Revolution or the United States War of Independence.

STAMP ACT: A tax passed by the British that forced the thirteen colonies to pay a tax on all printed papers. It was called the Stamp Act because an official stamp showed the tax had been paid. The Stamp Act angered the colonists—they felt the British did not have a right to tax them without giving them a vote in the British government.

TREASON: The crime of betraying one's country.

Selected Sources

Claghorn, Charles E. *Women Patriots of the American Revolution: A Biographical Dictionary.* Metuchen, NJ: Scarecrow Press, 1991.

Declaration of Independence. Printed by Mary Katharine Goddard. Baltimore, 1777. Continental Congress Broadside Collection. Library of Congress. loc.gov/resource/bdsdcc.02101/?sp=1.

Dvorak, Petula. "This Woman's Name Appears on the Declaration of Independence. So Why Don't We Know Her Story?" *Washington Post*, July 3, 2017. wapo.st/2sjDDIS.

Ham, Mary Katharine. "Meet the Only Woman with Her Name on an Official Declaration of Independence." The Federalist, July 4, 2017. thefederalist.com/2017/07/04/meet-the-only-woman-with-her-name-on-an-official-declaration-of-independence.

Humphrey, Carol Sue. "Goddard, Mary Katherine." In *American National Biography*, edited by John A. Garraty and Mark C. Carnes, 136–37. Vol. 9. New York: Oxford University Press, 1999.

Miner, Ward L. *William Goddard, Newspaperman.* Durham, NC: Duke University Press, 1962.

Young, Christopher, J. "Mary K. Goddard: A Classical Republican in a Revolutionary Age." *Maryland Historical Magazine* 96, no. 1 (Spring 2001): 5–27. msa.maryland.gov/megafile/msa/speccol/sc5800/sc5881/000001/000000/000382/pdf/msa_sc_5881_1_382.pdf.

Zeinert, Karen. *Those Remarkable Women of the American Revolution.* Brookfield, CT: Millbrook Press, 1996.

M. K. Goddard